INSIDE THE NFL

CHICAGO BEARS

by Todd Kortemeier

Abdo & Daughters
MIDDLE GRADE NONFICTION

An imprint of Abdo Publishing
abdobooks.com

ABDOBOOKS.COM

Published by Abdo Publishing, a division of ABDO, PO Box 398166, Minneapolis, Minnesota 55439.

Printed in China.
052025
092025

THIS BOOK CONTAINS RECYCLED MATERIALS

Cover Photos: Robin Alam/Icon Sportswire/Getty Images (Caleb Williams); David Madison/Getty Images Sport/Getty Images (Walter Payton)
Interior Photos: Brandon Sloter/Getty Images Sport/Getty Images, 4–5, 63; Eduardo Munoz Alvarez/AP Images, 6; Paul Sancya/AP Images, 7, 61 (bottom right); Michael Reaves/Getty Images Sport/Getty Images, 8; Carlos Osorio/AP Images, 9; Abdo Publishing, 10–11, 58; Bettmann/Getty Images, 12–13, 15 (top), 22, 23, 32, 60 (bottom left); AP Images, 15 (bottom), 18–19, 20, 21, 24–25, 27, 31, 37; Bruce Bennett Studios/Getty Images Studios/Getty Images, 16; Vernon Biever/AP Images, 26; James Drake/Getty Images Sport/Getty Images, 28, 29, 60 (bottom right); Focus on Sport/Getty Images, 30; UPI/Bettmann Archive/Getty Images, 33, 60 (top); Peter Read Miller/AP Images, 34–35, 41; Bill Smith/Getty Images Sport/Getty Images, 36; Paul Spinelli/NFL Photos/AP Images, 38, 45; Andrew D. Bernstein/Getty Images Sport/Getty Images, 39; Paul Natkin/Getty Images Sport/Getty Images, 40; Lennox McLendon/AP Images, 42; Rich Pilling/Diamond Images/Getty Images, 43; Focus on Sport/Getty Images Sport/Getty Images, 44, 46–47, 61 (bottom left); David Stluka/AP Images, 49; Alex Brandon/AP Images, 50; Al Messerschmidt Archive/AP Images, 51; Doug Benc/Getty Images Sport/Getty Images, 52, 61 (top); Rick Osentoski/AP Images, 53; Greg Trott/AP Images, 54–55; Todd Rosenberg/Getty Images Sport/Getty Images, 56; Todd Rosenberg/AP Images, 59

Editor: Rebecca Higgins
Series Designer: Laura Graphenteen
Production Designer: Ryan Gale

Library of Congress Control Number: 2024948489

Publisher's Cataloging-in-Publication Data

Names: Kortemeier, Todd, author.
Title: Chicago Bears / by Todd Kortemeier
Description: Minneapolis, Minnesota: Abdo Publishing, 2026 | Series: Inside the NFL | Includes online resources and index.
Identifiers: ISBN 9781098296674 (lib. bdg.) | ISBN 9798384919193 (ebook)
Subjects: LCSH: Chicago Bears (Football team)--Juvenile literature. | National Football League--Juvenile literature. | Football teams--Juvenile literature. | American football--Juvenile literature.
Classification: DDC 796.333--dc23

CONTENTS

Chicago quarterback Caleb Williams drops back to pass against the Los Angeles Rams in a 2024 game.

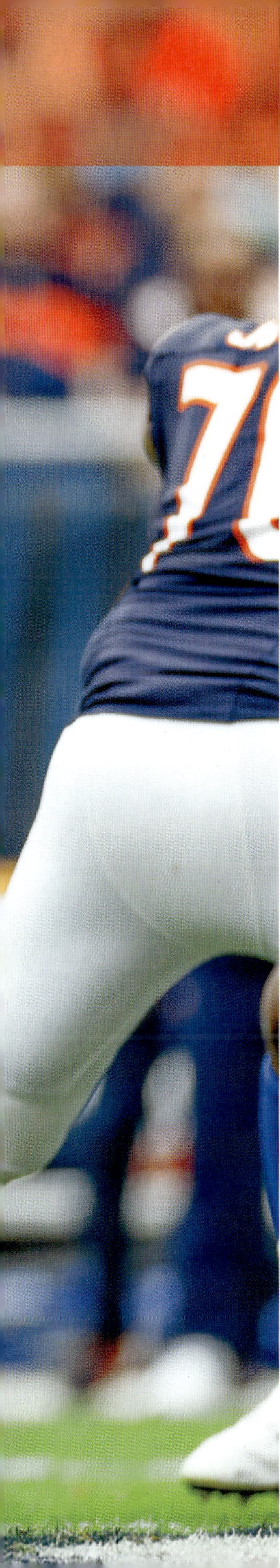

CHAPTER 1

WILLIAMS COMES ALIVE

Chicago Bears fans had reason to feel nervous. It was Week 5 of the 2024 National Football League (NFL) season, and their team had fallen behind the lowly Carolina Panthers early. But Bears fans also had a reason for hope.

That reason was Bears rookie quarterback Caleb Williams. He showed signs of progress, such as in Week 3 when he threw for 363 yards. That made him the first Bears rookie to throw for 300 yards in a game.

On the next possession against the Panthers, Williams marched his team down the field. On second down from the Panthers' 34-yard line, Williams faked a handoff to running back D'Andre Swift. Then he calmly scanned the defense. To his right, he saw star receiver D. J. Moore running wide-open toward the sideline. Williams hit

Moore perfectly with a pass. Moore then tiptoed his way down the sideline to stay inbounds and skipped into the end zone to tie the game 7–7.

After the previous week's game, Williams had been frustrated. Despite beating the Los Angeles Rams, Williams had failed to connect with Moore on what could have been a touchdown late in the first half. It was one of several mistakes the quarterback had made early in the season. Finding Moore for a big play against the Panthers was a promising sign for the rookie.

A NEW ERA

Williams was just beginning his NFL career. But it had been clear for a long time that he was destined for NFL stardom. At the University of Southern California in 2022, the quarterback had a historic season, setting school records for passing yards, total touchdowns, and completions.

Williams holds up the Heisman Trophy after winning the award in December 2022.

Prior to Williams, the Bears' last number one overall draft pick was running back Bob Fenimore in 1947.

Williams was awarded the Heisman Trophy as the best player in college football.

If Williams had been able to enter the 2023 draft, he likely would have been the number one pick. But NFL rules required him to play one more year of college football. In 2023, he did not play as well as his Heisman-winning season. Still, his explosive arm, ability to throw on the run, and accuracy kept him atop the draft-prospect rankings.

The Bears owned the first pick in the 2024 draft. Williams had everything the team was looking for. Over the years, Chicago had sent more players to the Hall of Fame than any other team. But only one, Sid Luckman, was a quarterback. And he retired in 1950. The Bears never had a quarterback pass for 4,000 yards in a season, which 10 NFL teams had in the 2023 season alone. Bears fans hoped that Williams would become a star quarterback and end their decades-long streak without a championship.

PILING UP YARDS

Late in the second quarter against the Panthers, Williams and Moore made another connection. Williams took the snap at the Carolina 30-yard line. He dropped back and saw Moore streaking up the middle of the field in great position to make the catch. Williams threw a pass right on target for Moore in the end zone. A Panthers defender tackled Moore just as he caught the pass, but he held on tight. The Bears scored their third touchdown of the second quarter to lead 27–7.

The Bears held on to their lead to secure a 36–10 victory. Moore caught both of Williams's passing touchdowns. In total, the quarterback threw for 304 yards. Williams became the first Bears rookie to pass for 300 yards without throwing an interception.

The matchup against the Panthers was the breakout game fans were looking for. Chicago cheered

CAROLINA CONNECTION

Caleb Williams might have joined another team if not for a Bears trade made before the 2023 draft. Chicago held the top pick that year but chose to trade the pick to Carolina for D. J. Moore and five other draft choices, including the Panthers' top pick in 2024. That pick turned out to be the first overall selection, and Chicago used it to choose Williams.

Receiver D. J. Moore had 96 receptions for 1,364 yards and eight touchdowns during his first season with the Bears in 2023.

on Williams, hopeful that he was on his way to stardom. Fans also hoped that someday Williams would lead the Bears to a Super Bowl victory.

NFL TEAMS MAP

NFC

NFC EAST

- DALLAS COWBOYS
- NEW YORK GIANTS
- PHILADELPHIA EAGLES
- WASHINGTON COMMANDERS

NFC WEST

- ARIZONA CARDINALS
- LOS ANGELES RAMS
- SAN FRANCISCO 49ERS
- SEATTLE SEAHAWKS

NFC NORTH

- CHICAGO BEARS
- DETROIT LIONS
- GREEN BAY PACKERS
- MINNESOTA VIKINGS

NFC SOUTH

- ATLANTA FALCONS
- CAROLINA PANTHERS
- NEW ORLEANS SAINTS
- TAMPA BAY BUCCANEERS

AFC

AFC EAST

- BUFFALO BILLS
- MIAMI DOLPHINS
- NEW ENGLAND PATRIOTS
- NEW YORK JETS

AFC WEST

- DENVER BRONCOS
- KANSAS CITY CHIEFS
- LAS VEGAS RAIDERS
- LOS ANGELES CHARGERS

AFC NORTH

- BALTIMORE RAVENS
- CINCINNATI BENGALS
- CLEVELAND BROWNS
- PITTSBURGH STEELERS

AFC SOUTH

- HOUSTON TEXANS
- INDIANAPOLIS COLTS
- JACKSONVILLE JAGUARS
- TENNESSEE TITANS

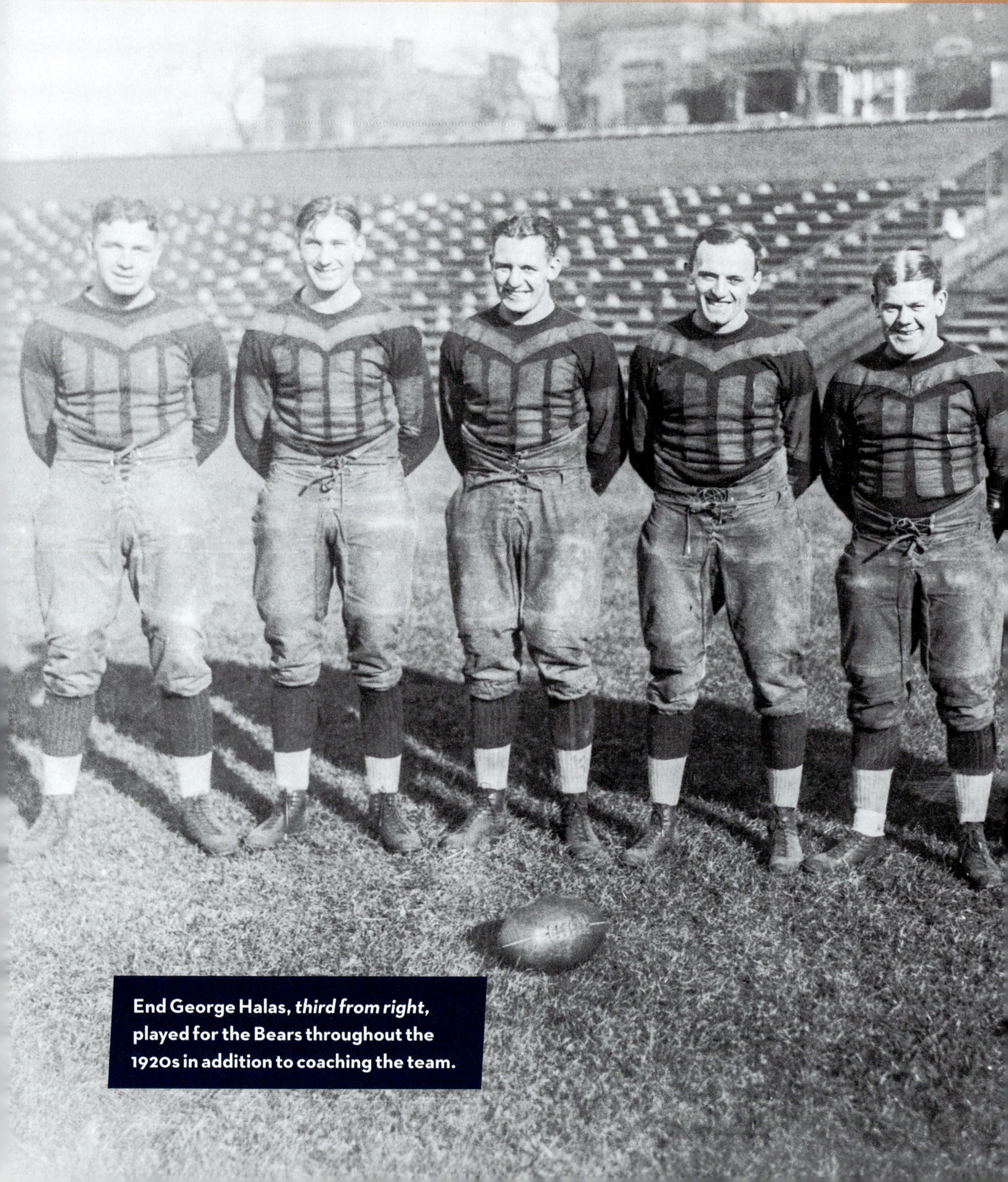

End George Halas, *third from right*, played for the Bears throughout the 1920s in addition to coaching the team.

CHAPTER 2

MONSTERS OF THE MIDWAY

According to the Bears' fight song, "Bear Down, Chicago Bears," the team is the "pride and joy of Illinois." The team has always represented the Land of Lincoln. But the franchise didn't begin in Chicago. And it wasn't always known as the Bears.

A. E. Staley, owner of the Staley Manufacturing Company in Decatur, Illinois, started a football team for his employees in 1919. Before the NFL, most football teams were made up of amateur athletes who mostly played for their regional team. Staley's company team, known as the Decatur Staleys, soon became one of the best in central Illinois. But Staley had bigger goals for his team.

In 1920, Staley hired George Halas to both play for and coach Decatur. That year, Halas led the Staleys as they joined a new league called the

American Professional Football Association (APFA). To draw more fans, the Staleys moved north to Chicago in 1921. Staley stayed behind in Decatur. He turned control of the team over to Halas.

Halas promised to keep the Staleys name for one year, and that year was a good one. The Chicago Staleys won the APFA championship in 1921. The league soon changed its name to the NFL and Halas chose a new nickname for his team. It was based on the team's home stadium, Wrigley Field, which it shared with baseball's Chicago Cubs. Halas reasoned that football players are often bigger and stronger than baseball players, so "Bears" was a fitting nickname. Halas was also responsible for choosing the team's blue and orange colors, which were inspired by his school, the University of Illinois.

EARLY INNOVATIONS

Halas was a good player and coach, but he had an even bigger impact off the field as the team's owner and executive. He led the Bears as they became the first team to practice every day, to study film of their opponents, and to have their games broadcast on the radio. In 1922, Chicago became the first team to "buy" a player from another team, paying the Rock Island Independents $100, or roughly $1,879 in 2025 money, for Ed Healy.

Today, most of college football's best players join the NFL. In the 1920s, few college stars turned pro. The league wasn't that well known, and many fans were more interested in college football. That began to change in 1925, when Halas signed star running back Red Grange from the University of Illinois. Grange was a sensation, and his signing validated the young league. Fans packed Wrigley Field to see Grange play. The Bears also filled visiting stadiums because of Grange.

Bears running back Red Grange was nicknamed "the Galloping Ghost" for his elusive running style.

Grange was still one of Chicago's top players in 1930. But that year, Halas added another attraction. Bronko Nagurski had starred at the University of Minnesota. He joined Grange in the backfield and also played on Chicago's defense. A muscular 6 feet, 2 inches, and 226 pounds, Nagurski was one of the most hard-nosed players in football. The dynamic duo of Grange and Nagurski was at its best in 1932.

At the time, the NFL champion was the team with the best winning percentage. Tied games weren't calculated into that number.

Fullback Bronko Nagurski, *right*, teamed with Grange, *left*, to form a dynamic backfield duo for the Bears.

Despite the 1932 Green Bay Packers having a 10–3 record, the Bears and Portsmouth Spartans tied for first place in the championship standings with matching 6-1-6 records. Rather than have the teams tie for first place, the league decided to hold a one-game battle for the title. The matchup was supposed to be played at Wrigley, but a severe snowstorm hit Chicago. Unable to play outside, the game was moved to Chicago Stadium, home of hockey's Chicago Blackhawks. For the first time, an NFL game was played indoors.

It was a strange setting. Since a football field is larger than a hockey rink, there was only room for an 80-yard field with two 10-yard end zones. There was no way to bring in grass—and artificial turf had yet to be invented—so the Bears and Spartans played on eight inches (20.3 cm) of dirt atop a concrete floor.

Guard/linebacker Dan Fortmann was a six-time first-team All-Pro for the Bears in the 1930s and 1940s while also studying to be a doctor in the offseason.

The game remained scoreless until late in the fourth quarter. Chicago drove to the Spartans' 2-yard line. On fourth down, Nagurski attempted to burst through the line and into the end zone. But with no way through, he stopped, backed up, jumped into the air, and threw a pass to the end zone. Grange hauled it in for the game's only score.

It wasn't an official championship game at the time, but the Bears' victory was enough to take the 1932 title. And despite the strange nature of the game, the NFL owners liked the idea. Before the 1933 season, they decided to split the league into two divisions. At the end of each year, the two division winners would compete for the championship.

SAVIORS AND SNEAKERS

The Bears won the 1932 title without Halas. He had stepped away from coaching in 1930 to focus solely on his role as owner. But he returned to the sideline in 1933 as the Bears looked to repeat as champions. They faced off against the New York Giants in the first official championship game.

At Wrigley Field, Nagurski threw a third-quarter touchdown to give Chicago a 16–14 lead. But the Giants answered with a score of their own. Late in the fourth quarter, Nagurski took the handoff and sent the ball 14 yards to Bears end Bill Hewitt. With defenders trailing him, Hewitt fired off a 19-yard touchdown pass for a 23–21 lead.

However, the Giants were not done. They drove down to get in position to score a would-be game-winning touchdown. But Grange

made a key tackle on New York's last play, and Chicago claimed a second straight league crown.

> **"[GRANGE] HAD THE CHAMPION'S KNACK OF TURNING IN HIS GREATEST PERFORMANCES IN THE CLUTCH."**
>
> **—GEORGE HALAS**

Later, Halas said, "[Grange] had the champion's knack of turning in his greatest performances in the clutch."

The Bears stormed through the 1934 season with a 13-0 record and headed into a championship rematch with the Giants. But New York's frigid field was a tougher opponent than the Giants. Wearing cleats, the Bears could not get any traction on the frozen ground. New York's players slipped in the

Chicago running back Beattie Feathers, *left*, tries to break a tackle in a 1937 game against the New York Giants.

first half too. But after switching to basketball shoes at halftime, the Giants had a lot more success moving the ball. New York's 30–13 victory became known as "the Sneakers Game."

TO A "T"

The Bears reached one more championship game in the 1930s. While they lost the 1937 title 28–21 to Washington, they were forming the basis for their next championship era. At the time, the most common offensive formation was called "the single wing." The ball usually was snapped to one of the running backs, and passes were scarce. The quarterback didn't even touch the ball on most plays. But Halas had been consulting with University of Chicago coach Clark Shaughnessy on a new offensive formation that would revolutionize football.

The Bears' new offensive approach was called "the T formation" because the quarterback lined up behind the center. Three backs then lined up behind the quarterback in a straight line, forming a T shape. Out of this setup, the quarterback took the snap and could hand the ball off, throw it, or run it.

Halas and Shaughnessy did not invent the T formation. But they did develop the strategy and bring it to the NFL. The Bears had so much success that the T formation is even mentioned in their fight song.

To run the formation well, Halas turned to Sid Luckman. Initially, Luckman struggled with the T's complexity. For a while, Halas switched him to a different position. But Luckman got it right on his second try. He was a skilled passer who led the NFL in touchdowns three times during the 1940s.

GOOD LUCK

Sid Luckman remains one of the best statistical quarterbacks in Bears history. He set team records for games started as a quarterback, passing yards, and completions, all of which stood for more than 70 years after he retired. Luckman also won the first Most Valuable Player (MVP) Award for a Bears player. He won the award in 1943. No Bear won it again until 1977.

Quarterback Sid Luckman threw for more than 14,000 yards and tossed 137 touchdowns in 12 seasons with the Bears.

BECOMING MONSTERS

With Luckman at the helm in 1940, the Bears' new formation took the NFL by storm. Chicago went 8–3 during the regular season. One of the team's losses was a controversial 7–3 defeat to Washington. The Bears thought pass interference should have been called on the last play.

Washington owner George Preston Marshall had called the Bears "crybabies" for complaining about the call. Halas had Marshall's words hung up in the Bears' locker room for motivation. When the teams met again in the title game, Chicago took the field at Washington's Griffith Stadium out for revenge.

Chicago fullback Bill Osmanski races away from Washington defenders in the 1940 NFL Championship Game. Osmanski scored the game's first touchdown on a 68-yard run.

Chicago scored its first touchdown just 56 seconds into the game. The Bears poured it on from there. They led 28–0 at halftime. Chicago's defense intercepted eight passes. The Bears scored 11 touchdowns. Officials had to ask Chicago to stop kicking extra points. The kicks had gone into the crowd and fans kept the balls. By the fourth quarter, there was only one ball left. The Bears won 73–0. More than eighty years later, it was still the largest margin of victory in NFL history.

The Bears celebrate their 41–21 victory over Washington in the 1943 NFL Championship Game.

The lopsided win started a run in which the Bears played for five championships in seven seasons, winning four. They even picked up a new unofficial nickname. Fans had called the University of Chicago team "the Monsters of the Midway" after the neighborhood of the city where they practiced. After the Bears' dominant decade, they stole the nickname. It has stuck ever since.

Chicago accomplished much of this winning without Halas on the sideline. He left in 1942 to serve in the military during World War II (1939–1945). Halas returned in 1946 and led the team to another title. But that was the last successful season in the Midway for years.

Bears coach Hunk Anderson, *left*, talks with Luckman in 1944. Luckman volunteered to deliver supplies and personnel during the war but was still able to play for Chicago.

Clyde "Bulldog" Turner starred for the Bears from 1940 to 1952 as a center and linebacker.

CHAPTER 3

LEGENDS AND LOSSES

AS ONE OF THE NFL'S OLDEST TEAMS, THE BEARS ARE INVOLVED IN some of the sport's most legendary rivalries. They have smashed helmets with the Green Bay Packers since 1921 and the Detroit Lions since 1930. But the Bears' oldest rival is today's Arizona Cardinals. The teams first met in 1920, when both played in Chicago, and they continued to battle for dominance each year until the Cardinals moved away in 1959.

In 1947, the Cardinals ended the Bears' championship run that had lasted most of the decade. The Bears finished that year 8–4 but lost to the Cardinals twice. The Bears watched their crosstown rival represent the West Division in the title game, which the Cardinals won. The next season, the Bears took a 10–1 record into the final week of the season. But the Cardinals defeated the Bears 24-21 and won the division.

LEGENDARY PLAYERS

Heading into the 1950s, George Halas looked to a new generation of star players. But after Sid Luckman retired in 1950, Halas had trouble finding a consistent quarterback. In 1953, starter George Blanda was struggling. During one game against the San Francisco 49ers, Halas replaced Blanda with Willie Thrower. In doing so, Thrower became the NFL's first Black quarterback. However, it also proved to be his only game after he completed just three of eight passes.

End/defensive back Harlon Hill (87) was named the 1955 MVP by the Newspaper Enterprise Association.

In 1954, Chicago's quarterbacks had a new receiving target. Rookie Harlon Hill exploded into the NFL with 45 receptions for 1,124 yards and a league-high 12 touchdowns. He led the NFL again the next season with nine scores. Hill was one of the league's top players for the first few years of his career. Then injuries took their toll on Hill.

George Connor was a dominant left tackle on offense and a fierce hitter as a linebacker. Though his career was cut short by injury in 1956, Connor helped establish Chicago's tradition of strong linebacking play. When Connor retired, Bill George moved back from his defensive line spot to play middle linebacker. He was named to the All-Pro team eight times between 1955 and 1963.

The Bears had winning records in all but three years between 1950 and 1959. But in an era when only one team from each division went to the postseason, Chicago reached the title game only once. That came in 1956, when they faced the Giants. On another icy day in New York, the Bears lost 47–7. Just as they had two decades earlier, the Giants came out wearing sneakers while the Bears did not.

Bill George is considered one of the pioneers of the middle linebacker position in the NFL.

HALAS'S LAST RUN

Halas didn't coach the 1956 championship game loss to the Giants. He had

George Halas, *center*, coached the Bears in five different decades.

once again stepped back from coaching to focus on ownership. But he returned in 1958. By 1963, he had the Bears on top again. Chicago finished 11–1–2 behind the passing combination of quarterback Billy Wade and tight end Mike Ditka. At the time, most tight ends were simply extra blockers, but the 24-year-old Ditka was a top receiver. He caught 59 passes and eight touchdowns, both team highs.

Chicago's bigger strength was its incredible defense. The Bears dominated opposing offenses, allowing just 17 touchdowns in 14 games. George led the way from his middle linebacker spot. Defensive backs Rosey Taylor, Richie Petitbon, and Bennie McRae had a combined total of 23 interceptions. "We had a heck of a football team," said Ditka.

Once again, the Bears faced the Giants in the title game. New York's league-leading offense was led by veteran quarterback Y. A. Tittle. The Giants led 10–7 at halftime, but Wade threw a key third-quarter pass to Ditka to get the Bears down near the Giants' goal line. Wade then snuck in his second touchdown of the day for a 14–10 lead.

Chicago's defense did the rest. The Bears intercepted Tittle five times. The final pick came from Petitbon, who pulled in a pass in the Chicago end zone in the final seconds to seal the win. Halas had his first championship in 17 years. He left the field immediately. As long as he had been a coach in the NFL, Halas never shook hands with the opposing coach after a game. He didn't see the point of coaches shaking hands because the losing one would be upset.

Tight end Mike Ditka, *left*, and quarterback Billy Wade walk off the field after the Bears' 14–10 win over the New York Giants in the 1963 league championship game.

Linebacker Dick Butkus was enshrined in the Pro Football Hall of Fame in 1979.

THE ANIMAL AND THE KANSAS COMET

Halas coached the team for four more seasons before moving to the owner's suite for good. He drafted two more superstars with consecutive picks in the 1965 draft. Linebacker Dick Butkus and running back Gale Sayers could not have been more different as players. But both shared the eternal love of Chicago's football fans.

Butkus was one of the most feared linebackers of all time. A Chicago native and star at the University of Illinois, Butkus was a beloved hometown hero. "The Animal" was a violent tackler but also had the speed and athleticism to chase down anyone on the field. An opposing running back once said he'd rather play against a grizzly bear than Butkus.

While Butkus was known for brute strength, Sayers had remarkable grace. When sprinting, Sayers reminded some of a ballet dancer more than a football player. But he was also a powerful runner, capable of trampling anyone in his path. Sayers didn't ask his blockers to open up big holes. "Give me 18 inches of daylight. That's all I need," he once said.

> ***"GIVE ME 18 INCHES OF DAYLIGHT. THAT'S ALL I NEED."***
>
> ***—GALE SAYERS***

Sayers announced himself to the NFL late in his rookie season. Despite playing on a muddy Wrigley Field on December 12, 1965, "the Kansas Comet" soared into the NFL record books. Early in the game, Sayers pulled in a screen pass from quarterback Rudy Bukich and sprinted 80 yards for a touchdown. By the end of the first half, he'd added rushing scores from 21 yards and 7 yards.

Sayers added his longest rushing score of the game early in the third quarter with a 50-yard dash. After scoring his fifth touchdown on a 1-yard run later in the third, he capped off his day on special teams. With the Bears up 47–20 in the fourth quarter, Sayers fielded a punt at his own 15. He ran to the right and slipped a tackle before galloping back across the field, shaking off two more defenders and bursting down the sideline for an 85-yard touchdown. His sixth score of the day tied the NFL record.

Running back Gale Sayers led the NFL in rushing yards in both 1966 and 1969.

In 1968, Sayers suffered a serious knee injury in a game. He returned the next year, but he was never the same player. He retired after the 1971 season having racked up 4,956 career rushing yards in just 68 games.

Butkus's career lasted longer, though he endured severe pain during his last three seasons.

After winning two NFL Defensive Player of the Year Awards and leading the Bears in tackles for eight straight years, Butkus injured his right knee in 1970. He had surgery to fix it, but his knee never fully healed. He still managed to make the Pro Bowl in 1971 and 1972 before retiring after the 1973 season.

Neither Sayers nor Butkus ever played in a postseason game for the Bears. But both lasted long enough to move the team into a new home. Soldier Field itself wasn't new. It had stood on Chicago's lakefront since 1924. The Bears moved in before the 1971 season. Though it would take time, the league's oldest stadium would soon house a new group of Bears legends, and the most memorable season the franchise had ever seen.

BRIAN'S SONG

In 1970, the Bears suffered a tragic loss as running back Brian Piccolo died of cancer at just 26 years old. The loss was especially great for Gale Sayers, who was very close friends with Piccolo. In 1971, the story of their friendship was told in an award-winning television movie called "Brian's Song." The story was popular even among those who were not Bears fans. Fifty-five million people tuned in to watch, which was roughly half of all people in the United States who owned televisions at the time.

Running back Brian Piccolo played for the Bears from 1966 until 1969.

Navy members form an American flag at Soldier Field. Soldier Field has been the Bears' home since 1971. The interior was rebuilt in 2002.

In 1999, the NFL named its Man of the Year Award after Chicago running back Walter Payton.

CHAPTER 4

SUPER BOWL SHUFFLING

For more than five decades, George Halas did basically everything for the Chicago Bears. But as Halas aged, he gave up some of his control. In 1974, he hired Jim Finks as executive vice president and general manager. One of Finks's main jobs was to draft the Bears' next generation of stars.

A year later, Finks eyed a running back from Jackson State named Walter Payton and selected him with the team's first-round pick. Starting in 1975, Payton missed only one game until 1987. But Payton wasn't just durable. He was an electrifying runner. "Sweetness" was capable of twirling around oncoming tacklers and barreling over others, sometimes on the same play. He could catch passes out of the backfield, protect quarterbacks as a powerful blocker, and even throw. Payton threw eight touchdown passes in his career.

COACHING DRAMA

Payton breaks free during his record-setting game against the Minnesota Vikings in 1977.

Payton led the National Football Conference (NFC) in rushing every year from 1976 to 1980. He led the entire NFL in 1977. That year he racked up 1,852 yards. In one game against the Minnesota Vikings, Payton smashed the NFL record by rushing for 275 yards in one game. Payton's MVP season led the Bears back to the playoffs for the first time in 14 years. But Chicago lost its first game.

The Bears went back to the playoffs in 1979 but lost their opener again. By 1982, Payton had been one of the NFL's most popular players for seven years, but he had never won a postseason game. Halas and Finks decided the Bears needed a new head coach. Many of the Bears' defensive players wanted Buddy Ryan to stay on as an assistant coach. With Finks's draft picks such as defensive tackle

Dan Hampton and middle linebacker Mike Singletary leading the way, Ryan's innovative "46" defense became one of the best in the league. The complicated scheme was designed around both stuffing the run and blitzing opposing quarterbacks on passing downs. Bears fans loved the team's improved defensive play, and the defensive players loved Ryan.

Linebacker Mike Singletary was the NFL's Defensive Player of the Year in 1985 and 1988.

Halas instead hired former Bears tight end Mike Ditka. Finks was upset that he wasn't consulted on the decision and eventually quit. The combative Ryan stayed on as defensive coordinator, forming an uneasy partnership with the equally feisty Ditka.

Despite the sometimes-tense atmosphere, the new coach was confident he could win in Chicago. "Give me three years," Ditka said upon meeting his players for the first time. "And if you walk with me, we'll get to the dance."

> ***"GIVE ME THREE YEARS. AND IF YOU WALK WITH ME, WE'LL GET TO THE DANCE."***
>
> ***—MIKE DITKA***

Sadly, Halas didn't live long enough to see that happen. He died at the age of 88 in 1983. Not only was "Papa Bear" the eternal face of football in Chicago, but he had also helped shape the NFL for six decades. Halas was honored around the league. The Bears added his initials "GSH" to their uniform sleeves as a tribute. Those letters still appear on Chicago uniforms today.

Tackle Steve McMichael was an All-Pro twice during his 13 seasons with the Bears after joining the team in 1981.

A MEMORABLE TEAM

In 1984, Ditka's Bears came within one game of the Super Bowl before losing to the San Francisco 49ers. The team returned in 1985 ready to dominate. The Bears' defense struck fear into its opponents. The new Monsters of the Midway hit hard and played with a ferocious streak that was reflected in the players' nicknames. Defensive end Steve McMichael was known as "Mongo" after a violent character in the 1974 movie *Blazing Saddles*. He played next to Hall of Famers Dan "Danimal" Hampton and Richard "Sackman" Dent. Mike Singletary was "Iron Mike." Outside linebacker Otis Wilson was "the Junkyard Dog." Safety Gary Fencik's nickname was "Hit Man."

The offense was led by a character of its own. Quarterback Jim McMahon seemingly didn't listen to anyone. He frequently changed Ditka's plays, which infuriated his coach. McMahon even took on the NFL's commissioner, Pete Rozelle. When the commissioner asked McMahon to stop wearing a headband sponsored by a company that wasn't affiliated with the league, McMahon got creative. He showed up at the next game wearing a new band with "Rozelle" written in black marker.

McMahon was also a tough leader, but the Bears' offense was still paced by the classy, humble Payton. He rushed for 1,551 yards and nine touchdowns in 1985. The Bears had the second-ranked scoring offense in the NFL that year. But Ryan's defense stole the show. The Bears smothered opponents like few defenses before them. Dent led the league with 17 sacks and seven forced fumbles.

Jim McMahon didn't put up big statistical numbers, but the Bears went 46–15 when he was the team's starting quarterback.

Chicago intercepted 34 passes and returned four of them for touchdowns. Meanwhile, the Bears allowed only 22 touchdowns all season.

TOTAL DOMINATION

The Bears toyed with opponents during the regular season as they started 12–0. Along the way, Ditka began sending defensive tackle William Perry in as a fullback for goal-line plays. Known as "the Refrigerator" for his massive 345-pound frame, the rookie powered his way to three touchdowns that season while becoming a fan favorite in Chicago.

The Bears finally lost in Week 13 against the Miami Dolphins on *Monday Night Football*. But the defeat didn't hamper Chicago's confidence. The next day, the players entered a music studio and recorded "The Super Bowl Shuffle." The song, which was

"The Super Bowl Shuffle" rose as high as number 41 on the *Billboard* music charts after it was released.

Bears defenders Wilber Marshall (58) and Dan Hampton (99) bring down a Los Angeles Rams running back during the NFC Championship Game on January 12, 1986.

intended to aid various Chicago charities, became a huge hit and was even nominated for a Grammy Award. "We love to play for the world's best fans," sang Dent. "You better start making your Super Bowl plans." That seemed very likely as the Bears won their next three games to finish 15–1.

The team's dominance continued in the playoffs. In the divisional round, Chicago held the New York Giants to just 181 total yards in a shutout win. The Bears were even better in the conference title game against the Los Angeles Rams, allowing just 130 yards in another shutout. No NFL team had ever shut out two teams in a single playoff campaign.

Defensive end Richard Dent (95) sacks New England Patriots quarterback Steve Grogan during Super Bowl XX on January 26, 1986.

SUPER FINISH

In January 1986, the Bears and their fans descended on New Orleans for Super Bowl XX. They were ready to celebrate a championship. Not many football fans around the country gave the underdog New England Patriots much of a chance.

Chicago's shutout streak ended early in the game. New England recovered a fumble by Payton on the game's second play and kicked a field goal four plays later. It proved to be one of the few highlights for New England.

Ryan's defense attacked Patriots quarterbacks Tony Eason and Steve Grogan all game. Eason, the starter, didn't complete any of his six passes, was sacked three times, and lost a fumble. The Bears picked off Grogan twice and sacked him four times. Chicago allowed positive yardage on just one of New England's first 16 plays. By halftime, the Bears were up 23–3 and cruising.

Chicago led 37–3 late in the third quarter and had the ball at the New England 1. Perry came on for a finishing touchdown. After the handoff, Perry met New England linebacker Larry McGrew head-on. The 233-pound McGrew went flying backward, and Perry scored one of the most famous touchdowns in Super Bowl history. Years later, however, Ditka regretted the decision. He didn't mind scoring but wished he'd called a play for Payton, who had been Chicago's heart and soul for a decade. Chicago went on to win 46–10, but Payton finished without a touchdown.

In the moment, however, the Bears were jubilant. At that time, it was common for coaches to be carried off the field after Super Bowl victories. The Bears hoisted two coaches. Some players went

Defensive tackle and end William "the Refrigerator" Perry blasts into the end zone in the third quarter of Super Bowl XX.

Mike Ditka, *center,* is carried off the field after the Bears' win in Super Bowl XX.

for Ditka. But the defensive unit also made sure Ryan got his own ride to the locker room. It was the final game in Chicago for the beloved defensive coach, who was about to be hired as the head coach of the Philadelphia Eagles.

The next day, the Bears were greeted by 500,000 fans in downtown Chicago as they held a championship parade. Even decades later, the 1985 Bears remain one of the most beloved teams in Chicago sports history. Their great play and colorful personalities amazed millions of fans.

SUPER BOWL AFTERMATH

The Bears remained a strong team in the years that followed Super Bowl XX. Chicago made playoff appearances in 1987 and 1988. But they couldn't make it back to the big game.

Perhaps the biggest reason for the Bears' decline was Payton's retirement after the 1987 season. Though he was still one of the top running backs in the NFL, Payton wanted to retire before his skills declined. He left the league as its all-time leading rusher and one of the most respected players ever.

By the early 1990s, much of the Bears' Super Bowl core was gone. After a 5–11 season in 1992, Ditka was fired, bringing an end to one of the greatest eras in Bears football. While the memories were still strong, the Bears had a long way to go to reach the Super Bowl again.

THE FOG BOWL

In 1988, Chicago met the Philadelphia Eagles in the playoffs. Mike Ditka and his Bears competed against their former assistant coach, Buddy Ryan. But the game became best known for the heavy fog that covered Soldier Field. It was so thick that fans and even TV cameras could barely make out the field. Players struggled to even see one another. The Bears managed through the fog better than the Eagles in a 20–12 win.

Chicago wide receiver Dennis Gentry tries to make a move during "the Fog Bowl" in December 1988.

Chicago quarterback Erik Kramer looks to make a pass against the Minnesota Vikings in 1995.

CHAPTER 5

THE QUARTERBACK SEARCH

By 1995, Bears legend Sid Luckman had been retired for 45 years. And though the quarterback played in an era when football was much more of a running game, many of his Bears passing records still stood. Only one quarterback had topped his 2,712 yards in the 1947 season, and no one had thrown more than Luckman's 28 touchdowns in 1943.

Chicago quarterback Erik Kramer tossed his 29th touchdown pass of the 1995 season in Week 16 against the Philadelphia Eagles. He also set a new team yardage mark of 3,838. Bears fans hoped they finally had a superstar quarterback to lead them back to glory. But Kramer struggled with injuries and never reached that level again.

Without a consistent signal-caller, the Bears stumbled through the 1990s. After Mike Ditka's firing in 1992, Chicago posted only two winning records for the rest of the decade. As 2001 dawned, not many thought the Bears would improve much from their 5–11 season the year before.

However, the 2001 Bears followed the recipe of the 1985 team. Running back Anthony "A-Train" Thomas rushed for 1,183 yards and seven touchdowns and won the Offensive Rookie of the Year Award. The team's top-ranked defense was paced by All-Pro defensive tackle Ted Washington and safety Mike Brown, as well as the Bears' newest star at middle linebacker.

Brian Urlacher had been Chicago's top draft pick in 2000. He won the league's Defensive Rookie of the Year Award that season. Urlacher soon became a fan favorite as he continued the tradition set by Dick Butkus and Mike Singletary. Similar to the two legends, Urlacher was an athletic and physical player. He also was known for his intelligence and vision on the field. Urlacher had a talent for knowing where the play was going and how to get in perfect position. "I think he's the greatest linebacker in team history," said teammate Alex Brown. "That says a lot."

Chicago finished 13–3 as the defense allowed just 12.7 points per game. But the Bears were

BROWN DELIVERS

In Week 6 of the 2001 season, the Bears went to overtime tied 31–31 with the San Francisco 49ers. Just six seconds into the extra session, Chicago safety Mike Brown intercepted a pass and returned it 33 yards for the winning score. A week later, Brown intercepted an overtime pass against the Cleveland Browns. He returned it 16 yards for another game winner. Brown was the first player in league history to win back-to-back overtime games on defensive touchdowns.

"I THINK HE'S THE GREATEST LINEBACKER IN TEAM HISTORY."

—ALEX BROWN ON BRIAN URLACHER

Safety Mike Brown scored seven defensive touchdowns in nine seasons with the Bears between 2000 and 2008.

undone by their poor quarterbacking in the playoffs. In the divisional round, journeymen Jim Miller and Shane Matthews totaled just 89 yards and three interceptions in a 33–19 loss to the Eagles.

A "LOVE" OF DEFENSE

Rex Grossman was the Bears' next quarterback hope. The strong-armed Grossman was the team's first-round pick in 2003. But he struggled to get on the field in his first three seasons, starting only seven games. Finally, in 2006, coach Lovie Smith handed Grossman the starting job.

The inconsistent Grossman threw 23 touchdown passes but also 20 interceptions. But Chicago had a strong running game with backs Thomas Jones and Cedric Benson, and Smith's defense often came to the rescue. The Bears also had their special teams weapon, All-Pro rookie Devin Hester. In Week 14, the punt returner and wide receiver returned a kickoff 96 yards for a score. "Devin Hester, you are ridiculous!" said Jeff Joniak on the Bears' radio call.

Urlacher was joined by star outside linebacker Lance Briggs. Charles "Peanut" Tillman was developing into a top cornerback. Tillman had a knack for forcing fumbles. After squaring up a ball carrier, he would make a fist and punch at the ball, often knocking it loose. Using "the Peanut Punch," Tillman forced 42 fumbles in 12 seasons with the Bears. Behind those stars, the 2006 Bears held opponents to just 15.9 points per game.

Chicago running back Thomas Jones scores his second touchdown of the NFC Championship Game against the New Orleans Saints in January 2007.

Chicago finished 12–4 and claimed the NFC North Division. Clutch kicker Robbie Gould came up big in the playoffs. He kicked a game-tying 41-yard field goal with 4:24 left in the division round against the Seattle Seahawks. Gould then won it 27–24 in overtime on a 49-yard kick. In the NFC title game the next week, Jones rushed for 123 yards and two touchdowns in a 39–14 rout of the New Orleans Saints. The Bears were headed back to the Super Bowl for the first time since the magical 1985 season.

Chicago started Super Bowl XLI against the Indianapolis Colts by unleashing Hester. He had returned three punts and two kickoffs for touchdowns that season. Hester didn't hold back in the big game.

Linebacker Brian Urlacher led the Bears with 142 sacks during the 2006 team's run to the Super Bowl.

He snagged the opening kick against the Colts on the left side of the field. Using his blazing speed, Hester cut across the field before spotting an opening and racing 92 yards for a touchdown.

Hester's return was one of few highlights for the Bears. Grossman threw two interceptions and lost a fumble. The Bears' defense kept it close, but Chicago lost 29–17.

QUARTERBACK CAROUSEL

Grossman started only eight more games in two seasons for the Bears. He was replaced by the rocket-armed Jay Cutler, who was acquired in a trade with the Denver Broncos. Cutler was a gambling quarterback, capable of tossing seemingly impossible passes. But he often took risks that frustrated coaches and fans.

Cutler was good enough in 2010 to lead Chicago to the NFC Championship Game. There, Chicago hosted the Green Bay Packers. It was the first postseason meeting ever between two of the league's most storied teams. On a frigid day at Soldier Field, Cutler was injured in the first half. Backup Caleb Hanie came on and threw a key second-half interception as Chicago lost 21–14.

Receiver Devin Hester's touchdown on the opening kickoff was one of the few Bears highlights in Super Bowl XLI on February 4, 2007.

After starting for the Bears in 2016, Cutler lost that role partway through the season. He lasted long enough to break Luckman's franchise career records for passing yards and touchdowns, but he never again took Chicago to the playoffs. Cutler was released after the season.

The next hope for Chicago fans was the number two pick in the 2017 draft, Mitchell Trubisky. Trubisky was a risky pick. He had started only a handful of games in college. But in his second pro season, Trubisky guided Chicago to a 12–4 record. He completed 67 percent of his passes and threw 24 touchdowns on his way to the Pro Bowl.

Quarterback Jay Cutler broke Sid Luckman's team records for career passing yards and touchdown passes.

Chicago's playoff stay was brief and painful. Trubisky threw for more than 300 yards and a touchdown, but Chicago lost 16–15 to the Eagles. In the final seconds, kicker Cody Parkey's potential game-winning

field-goal attempt hit the left upright, then bounced down off the crossbar and into the end zone. On television, commentator Cris Collinsworth infamously dubbed the kick "the Double Doink."

Quarterback Mitchell Trubisky made his only Pro Bowl after the 2018 season when he threw for 24 touchdowns.

Trubisky never lived up to the promise of the 2018 season. After struggling for two years, he was replaced by another first-round pick: Justin Fields. The former Ohio State star was an

Bears cornerback Jaylon Johnson makes an interception against the Las Vegas Raiders in 2023. Johnson reached the Pro Bowl after the 2023 and 2024 seasons.

electric runner. Fields scrambled for 1,143 yards in 2022. He was just the third NFL quarterback to ever top 1,000 rushing yards in a season. But Fields struggled as a passer. In three seasons with the dual-threat quarterback as a starter, the Bears were just 14–30.

THIS TIME IS THE CHARM?

Fields was traded to the Pittsburgh Steelers before the 2024 season. The Bears turned their hopes over to number one draft pick Caleb Williams. The Bears had used a first-round pick on a quarterback three times in the last eight years. But fans had reason to believe that they had finally found their franchise quarterback.

Williams had a stronger college career than Trubisky or Fields. He was widely considered the best quarterback in his draft. And while he could also run the ball, he was a strong passer with great accuracy.

The Bears also brought in some prime targets for him to throw to. In addition to already having D. J. Moore, the Bears drafted promising receiver Rome Odunze. Chicago also traded for star veteran Keenan Allen to give Williams more weapons.

Williams set a Bears' rookie record with 363 yards passing in his third game. Chicago lost, but Williams led the team to three straight victories. The Bears headed into their bye week 4–2. Many wondered whether the team was playoff ready. But Chicago lost its next game to the Washington Commanders on a final-play Hail Mary. The defeat kicked off a 10-game losing streak. After Chicago botched a potential game-winning drive in a Thanksgiving loss to the Detroit Lions, head coach Matt Eberflus was fired.

BEARS TROPHY CASE

SUPER BOWL CHAMPIONSHIPS: 1

Super Bowl XX – January 26, 1986

NFL CHAMPIONSHIPS: 8

1921, 1932, 1933, 1940, 1941, 1943, 1946, 1963

CONFERENCE CHAMPIONSHIPS: 2

1985, 2006

DIVISION TITLES: 19

1933, 1934, 1937, 1940, 1941, 1942, 1943, 1946, 1984, 1985, 1986, 1987, 1988, 1990, 2001, 2005, 2006, 2010, 2018

All stats are through the 2024 season.

Caleb Williams, *left*, and fellow rookie Rome Odunze, *right*, were both picked in the top 10 of the 2024 NFL Draft.

Despite the losses, Williams showed promise. Though often scrambling behind a struggling offensive line, he threw 20 touchdown passes and only six interceptions. He also passed for 3,541 yards, the fifth-highest total in the team's long history. Williams's first season was ultimately a disappointment, but Chicago hoped it had the quarterback to turn the team into the Monsters of the Midway once again.

TIMELINE

The Decatur Staleys are founded as an amateur football team.
1919

The Bears, known as "the Monsters of the Midway," beat Washington in a historic 73–0 win in the NFL Championship Game using their famous T formation.
1940

The Bears move from their longtime home of Wrigley Field to Soldier Field.
1971

1932
Led by star player Red Grange, the Bears win their first championship as members of the NFL.

1963
The Bears win their final championship of the pre-Super Bowl era, and the last one under coach George Halas.

1982
The Bears hire former player Mike Ditka as head coach.

Halas dies, leading the team to add his initials to their uniforms as a permanent tribute.
1983

Payton retires as the NFL's all-time leading rusher.
1987

Led by a new generation of defensive stars and kick returner Devin Hester, the Bears return to the Super Bowl but lose to the Indianapolis Colts on February 4.
2007

1986
Led by running back Walter Payton and a defense stocked with Hall of Famers, the Bears win their first Super Bowl on January 26 after a dominant 15–1 season.

2011
Veteran quarterback Jay Cutler leads the Bears to the conference title game on January 16, his only playoff appearance with the team.

2024
With the first pick in the draft, the Bears select quarterback Caleb Williams.

GLOSSARY

amateur–a person who plays a sport without getting paid.

backfield–the area on the field behind the line of scrimmage where the offensive players line up.

clutch–an important or pressure-packed situation.

commissioner–the chief executive of a sports league.

conference–a subset of teams within a sports league.

coordinator–an assistant coach who is in charge of the offense, defense, or special teams.

draft–a system that allows teams to acquire new players coming into the league.

dynamic–energetic and exciting; in sports, usually referring to an athlete with one or more outstanding skills.

favorite–the person or team that is expected to win.

franchise quarterback–a quarterback capable of leading a team for a number of years.

general manager–an executive who runs a team and is responsible for finding and signing players.

Hail Mary–a long pass that has a small chance of succeeding, usually made near the end of a game as a last-ditch effort to score.

Hall of Fame–the highest honor a player or coach can get when his or her career is over.

interception–a pass that is caught by a defensive player.

postseason–another word for playoffs; the time after the end of the regular season when teams play to determine a champion.

revolutionize—to change something in a significant way.

rookie—a professional athlete in his or her first year of competition.

special teams—the players on the field for kicking and punting plays.

upright—one of the two vertical poles on a goalpost.

veteran—someone who has played for many years.

ONLINE RESOURCES

Booklinks
NONFICTION NETWORK
FREE! ONLINE NONFICTION RESOURCES

To learn more about the Chicago Bears, please visit **abdobooklinks.com** or scan this QR code. These links are routinely monitored and updated to provide the most current information available.

INDEX